Know Your Employee and their Satisfaction

:: Author ::

GANESHBHAI C. NARBHAVAR

(M.COM., B.ED., G-SET)

PUBLISHED BY

The New Era International Publishing House
HQ. At & Po. Chaveli., Ta- Chansma,
Dist- Patan, North Gujarat, India, Asia.
www.iphouseindia.com

First Publication: 16th NOVEMBER, 2015

ISBN:- *978-1-51747-699-1*

Price: Rs.800/- INDIA

$ 15 OUTSIDE INDIA

PUBLISHED BY

**The New Era International Publishing House
HQ. At & Po. Chaveli., Ta- Chansma,
Dist- Patan, North Gujarat, India, Asia.
www.iphouseindia.com**

Dedicated

to

my

Parents

Knowing Your Employees - An Overview

Any individual who strives hard to accomplish goals and objectives of a particular organization is called as employee. Employees are hired to perform specific duties as per their specialization, interest areas and previous experiences. Employees earn their salaries in exchange for their hard work, labour, knowledge and expertise. It is rightly said that the success and failure of an organization depends on its employees. Employees are indeed the lifeline of an organization.

Management should know its employees well. *You need to understand your employees and what they expect from the organization? How can you ignore someone who spends his/her maximum part of the day at workplace?* Believe me, there are some organizations where managers don't even know the names of their subordinates. Organizations of such kind always face problems like employee dissatisfaction, high attrition rate and frequent conflicts among team members and eventually fail to do well in the long run. How would you feel if someone addresses you by a wrong name or simply by "Hey or Mr. or Ms"? It is an absolute insult to an employee who is addressed by a wrong name.

As a manager; you need to know some basic details of your employees. Yes, you need to memorize the names of all individuals who are directly/indirectly reporting to you, their expertise, background, capabilities etc.

Management spends most of its time and energy in knowing the target customers, then why not know your employees as well who are so important for your organization? Employees who feel ignored at the workplace seldom contribute to the success of an organization. Take out some time to sit with your team members to understand their expectations, interest levels, grievances or any other problems they face in their day to day operations and so on. It is important for the managers to connect with their team members. You ought to have the contact numbers of all your team members with you. Wish them on their birthdays and anniversaries to make them feel special. Trust me, knowing your employee not only strengthens your relationship with your team members but also make you a source of inspiration for them. Let your employees know that you care for them. Make them feel valued. Find out what is important to them, understand where they see themselves five years down the line, know in which all areas they can contribute their level best.

Knowing employees not only helps managers extract the best out of staff members but also motivates them to perform exceptionally well everytime. As a manager, it is your responsibility to assist them in their day to day operations and help them achieve their goals and targets. You need to know what your employees are upto? A manager must be aware of the key responsibility areas and job responsibilities of all his team members.

Knowing your employee also enables you to have a control on your subordinate. If you yourself don't know the job responsibilities of your team members, how can you expect them to respect and most importantly trust you. Find out whether they have any problems in the organization or not? Stand by them whenever they need your help. Managers need to acknowledge the hard work of their employees to expect a brilliant performance from them always. Knowing employees gives them a sense of recognition at the workplace. One feels proud to be a part of the organization and eventually delivers his/her level best.

Importance of Knowing Employees

Knowing employees plays a crucial role in motivating employees to deliver their level best. Knowing employees helps managers to understand their needs and expectations from the organization.

Managers need to know whether their team members are happy with their jobs or not? Do not make your employees feel ignored or left out. Believe me; they would hardly contribute towards the organization. Unless and until they feel themselves indispensable for the organization, they would never take things seriously. In such cases, individuals attend office just to receive their monthly pay checks and treat work as a mere source of burden.

Do you ever think of speaking ill of your family members, friends or relatives? Absolutely NO. Then why always criticize your BOSS? Why don't we feel like coming to our office whereas we enjoy so much at homes? Have you ever asked yourself?

Managers need to understand that employees need to be appreciated for them to perform consistently. Let them feel special. Problems arise when managers do not acknowledge the hard work of employees. Remember; you are not paid for just sitting in your cabin and passing on instructions to your team members. There are managers who do not even know their team members properly. Sit with your team members on a regular basis to know them, evaluate their work and provide correct feedbacks. As a manager, it is your responsibility to guide your team members and help them achieve their targets within the stipulated time frame. Know which all team members are actually contributing towards the organization and who all are just coming to have fun at work place? Appreciate employees who perform extraordinarily. Reward them suitably. Employees feel happy and proud to be a part of the organization when their performances are noticed.

Knowing employees well leads to a healthy work culture. When employees know each other well, they seldom fight and criticize fellow workers. Conflicts and misunderstandings not only spoil the ambience in the workplace but also increase the stress levels of individuals. Employees feel frustrated and find it extremely difficult to deliver results under such circumstances. Do not stop your employees from talking to individuals representing other departments. What is the problem if people have friends at the workplace? Everyone is mature enough to understand that there are certain things which are confidential and should not be disclosed. Team managers should also discuss an individual's family, his/her personal life, relatives and so on once in a while but yes, do not interfere too much in their personal lives. Do not ask something which is too personal for an employee. Employees feel happy when managers connect with them on a personal level. They feel like coming to work daily, face challenges with a smile and also constantly strive hard to take their organization to the top. Make your employees feel responsible for the organization. Let them understand that their projects or job responsibilities are just like their own babies and they need to be sincere and take good care of the same.

Managers need to know the names of all their team members and understand where all their team members are lacking and what all initiatives would make them a better professional. Knowing employees well leads to better results and better productivity. When managers understand their employees well and vice a versa, there is hardly any problem and organizations become a better place to work.

Know Your Employees to Improve Work Culture

Employees are indeed true assets of an organization. *Managers need to know their employees well to expect them to contribute their level best and also to remain loyal towards the organization*. Employees need to feel valued and important at the workplace for them to deliver their level best.

Knowing employees well leads to a healthy work culture. Managers connect with their team members and employees tend to know each other better. No individual can work in an organization where people do not talk to each other.

Human beings need people around to talk to and express their feelings. We spend the maximum part of our day at workplaces and it is essential for us to have friends here. Work becomes a mere source of burden when individuals are glued to their computers the whole day. Discussions and brainstorming sessions lead to innovative solutions and quick results.

Knowing employees strengthens the relationship between employees and their Bosses. Being rude to employees will not only demotivate them but also make you an unpopular member within the organization. Call them by their names rather than addressing as "Mr/Ms" or "Hey", greet them with a smile and enquire what is going on in their personal lives once in a while and see the difference yourself. Trust me; you will be elated to see employees striving hard to accomplish assigned targets within the shortest possible time frame.

Conflicts and misunderstandings lead to no solutions. Fights over petty issues not only lead to frustration but also spoil the ambience at the workplace. Do not forget that we are not school going kids who would fight over small things. It is essential to behave as mature professionals. Encourage healthy communication at workplace where employees get an opportunity to interact with each other, discuss ideas and also gain from each other's expertise. Let them open up. Knowing each other well leads to better understanding among employees and they seldom fight with each other, eventually leading to a healthy and positive work culture. It also leads to peace at the workplace. Knowing employees helps managers to understand how he can motivate his team members and use them to the best of their abilities. It helps you to understand which team member would fit into which particular role and which employee would not do justice to his work? Knowing employees helps you judge your subordinates well and hence there is no question of confusions at the workplace. There is seldom any overlapping of work and everyone knows what he/she is supposed to do? Individuals feel attached towards their organization and love coming to work.

Appreciate employees whenever they perform any extraordinary task. Praise them in front of all. Let him/her feel indispensable for the organization. This way, you are not only motivating the employee who has performed well but also others who have failed this time.

You need to keep a track on your employees' performances and give them correct feedback for them to perform as per expectations. Team members can also give each other suggestions to yield better results.

Improving Morale by Knowing Your Employees

Knowing your employees well acts as an essential morale booster and plays a crucial role in extracting the

best out of team members. Employees feel happy when their managers know them by their names and make them feel important. Employees tend to develop a sense of pride when their work gets noticed and appreciated by their Bosses. Managers should get along with their team members well and communicate with them effectively. Work suffers when employees feel left out at the workplace. Promote team work at workplace so that employees come together, share ideas and know each other better.

Managers ought to recognize the hard work of employees. Appreciate them whenever they perform any extraordinary task. This would not only motivate the employees who have performed well but also others who could not live up to the expectations this time. A manager needs to know who all employees have performed well and who all still need to pull up their socks.

Appreciating employees goes a long way in motivating employees and extracting the best out of them. A pat on their back is necessary to let them know that they are indispensable for the organization. Let them feel important. The moment, their work goes unnoticed they loose interest in work and attend office just for the sake of receiving paychecks. Knowing your employees and acknowledging their hard work inculcate a sense of pride and loyalty in individuals and they feel attached towards the organization. Employees must be given their share of the credit. There are organizations, where managers take away the whole credit. Such managers are always criticized and are never really liked by their team members. Small initiatives such as "Employee of the month", "Star Performer" and so on make employees feel special and motivate them to strive hard to perform even better.

Greet employees with a smile. Never be rude to them. Managers ought to address team members on a common platform so that no one feels ignored. Discuss critical issues in the presence of all to pass on information in its desired form. Individuals should have the liberty to express their views and come up with innovative ideas and solutions. Avoid being partial at the workplace. Each and every employee ought to be treated as one. Do not ignore someone just because he is not well -to- do. The moment you discourage someone to speak and express his/her views, he/she fails to perform.

Wish employees on their birthdays and anniversaries. You need to have contact numbers of all your team members. Do not hesitate to call if the other person is in trouble. You need to enquire about your team members' health, family, etc. Listen to their problems and try to give them solutions as well. Gone are the days when managers used to maintain a distance from their employees. Now a days it is essential for the supervisors to treat their employees with respect and understand them well. Do not treat your employees as mere slaves. Believe me; such an attitude will lead you nowhere.

What Do Employees Expect From Managers ?

It is essential for managers to know what their employees expect from them and the organization.

Let us find out what an employee expects from his managers and superiors:

Every individual is hungry for recognition. A manager needs to acknowledge the hard work of employees and appreciate them in front of others. This way, employees feel motivated to deliver better results and also feel attached towards the organization. Every employee expects his/her manager to praise him/her in front of other team members. Give them their due credit. Make them feel important. Put their names on notice boards, and reward them suitably. Money is a strong motivating factor for employees.

Every employee expects his/her superiors to be polite with him/her. Never shout on your team members. Being a Boss does not give you the authority to be rude with your subordinates. Lend a sympathetic ear to their problems and help them whenever possible.

Employees expect their managers to act as a strong pillar of support for them. As a manager, you need to stand by your team members under all circumstances. Trust me, employees feel happy if their superiors sit with them and assist them in their work. Motivate them to come up with innovative ideas and improvement solutions. Help them plan their day. Employees expect your guidance and mentoring. You need to be a strong leader who is capable of providing a direction to his team members.Help them meet their targets and accomplish tasks within the shortest possible time frame. Give them honest feedbacks. Suggest them new techniques, strategies which would help them not only in their current job but also in their future assignments.

Employees expect their managers to be their role models. You need to be a strong source of inspiration for them. Your team members would definitely copy your style, thus be very careful of what you wear at workplace. Create a style of your own which is unique.

Do not hesitate to give employees additional responsibilities provided you feel he/she is capable of performing a particular task. Make them accountable for various projects. Give them opportunities which would give them a chance to display their talent and creativity. Problems arise when employees start treating work as a mere source of burden. Employees feel frustrated when they do not have something new to work on.

Employees expect managers to interact with them. No one likes to work in an organization where they need to take permission to speak to their reporting bosses. How would you feel if your boss does not wish you on your Birthday? Yes, employees expect their reporting bosses to wish them at least on their special days. Greet your employees with a smile.

Be transparent with your employees. Do not be too rigid with them. Give them some freedom and liberty to take decisions on their own. Believe me; work will suffer if they have to take approvals for everything. Do not be after their lives for every small thing. Do not ask them to keep you in loop in every email. Let them handle situations on their own. Give them freedom to work in their own way.

Treat your employees as one. Never make fun of your team members.

Employees expect their salaries to be released on time. Never hold back their salaries or incentives. Sign their bills on time and do not ask for unnecessary explanations.

Mistakes Managers Make in Knowing Employees

Let us highlight some common mistakes managers make in knowing and managing employees:

Do not expect your team members to know everything. How can an individual perform each and every task with perfection? Key responsibility areas should not be designed just for the sake of it. Responsibilities should be delegated as per capabilities, specialization and interest areas of individuals. Do not impose unnecessary burden on employees. Trust me; they would not stick around for a long time. Managers need to master the art of extracting the best out of each employee by assigning work which interests him/her. Do not ask everyone to do everything. It will lead to a complete mess. Accept the fact that in only very rare circumstances, an individual can perfectly match all your specifications.

Yes, employees expect managers to connect on a personal level as well. Individuals feel motivated when their reporting boss enquires about their family, children or relatives. They speak high of their managers even if they are not around.

The common mistake which managers make in knowing employees is that they interfere too much in their personal lives. Problems arise when personal lives are discussed at the workplace. Please do not bring your personal problems to work. How would you feel if your Boss asks you about your affair? or something which is too personal. Managers should avoid discussing topics which have no relevance at the workplace. Too much of personal interference in anyone's life is not at all acceptable in organizations. Avoid being overfriendly with your team members. You will have difficulty in managing them as friendship is all about going out together, gossiping, and complaining about work and sometimes even Boss. Be warm and polite with them. Small get-togethers or snacks parties are excellent initiatives to know your employees but make sure you are not overdoing the same. Too much of parties also spoil the work culture and employees stop taking work seriously. Do not ask for undue favours from your team members.

Knowing employees does not mean that you will sit and gossip with your team members. Managers need to spend time with their subordinates to know what they are upto,to find out where they are lacking, in which all areas they can contribute more? and so on. Knowing employees helps managers to understand their capabilities, strong points, weaknesses etc. You do not have to waste your time by simply discussing things which are not related to work. Remember, your organization is paying you for your hard work, so please do not waste time unnecessarily, instead find out how you along with your team members can contribute more effectively towards your organization.

Even if you know everything about an employee, please *do not disclose internal policies and strategies which*

probably the top management has confided in you. You never know when the other individual backstabs you.

Managers feel addressing employees by their nick names would bring them closer to their team members. Sometimes it may go the other way round. Avoid calling them by their nicknames or surnames. They might feel bad. ***Call employees only by their first names***. Avoid slangs at workplace.

Encourage two way transparent communication at workplace.

Things Employees Hide from Managers

Why do you think employees lie to their managers and superiors? There are several instances when employees feel compelled to hide the truth from their seniors.

Let us go through some instances where the phrase "Honesty is the best policy" does not work.

An employee will never tell his manager that the targets imposed on him/her are unrealistic and impossible. Individuals have a tendency to say a yes to everything their boss asks them to do. You need to negotiate. If you feel something is not possible, speak up in the beginning itself if you do not wish to face the music later on. Managers should not set unrealistic targets for their team members. Unrealistic targets compel employees to speak lies to their reporting Bosses. Employees should have the liberty to express their opinions and views. If you feel your manager is being irrational, you have all the rights to correct him. Do not forget to be polite. Never ever be rude to anyone at the workplace.

Job responsibilities should be assigned to employees as per their specialization, interest areas and capabilities. Some employees do lie in order to get jobs, but as a manager you need to be smart enough to understand in what all situations an individual can hide the truth from you. Do not impose anything on your team members. The moment work becomes a burden for employees, they start lying.

Do not be after an employee's life to finish tasks. Competition is necessary to extract the best out of employees but be careful it should not lead to unnecessary pressure among employees. Employees lie when there is unnecessary work pressure on them. Give them enough time to complete their assignments provided the client does not want results in the shortest possible time frame.

Employees hide things from managers when managers do not share things with them. Remember as a manager, you need to be honest enough to expect honesty from your employees. It is essential to be transparent with your team members. Sit with your team members on a common platform; take their suggestions as well while formulating important strategies and policies. Employees should be very clear about the rules and regulations of the organization.

Managers ought to be sensible if they expect their team members to be honest with them. Do you think if you do not allow your subordinate to take a leave on his birthday, he would be honest to you in future? He would definitely find out some other excuse to take a leave on his special day. Be rational. Some days are special and no one likes to work on his/her birthday or anniversary.

Do not force your employees to make false commitments to customers. The moment you ask your employees to speak lies to customers, there is no guarantee that they would be honest to you also.

Managers should not interfere in any employee's personal life. Do not ask anything to your employees which is not related to their job. If you ask your team member whether he is going around with his female counterpart, do you think you will ever get an honest reply? Avoid personal talks at workplace. Office is not a place where you can discuss your affairs, personal problems, your dresses, jewellery and so on.

Employees will hide things from you if you adopt a "Hitler" like approach at the workplace. Employees tend to play with information if you are too strict with them. You need to deal with employees sensibly and in a mature way.

Things Managers Should Know About Their Employees

It is essential for a manager to know his/her team members well to understand their strengths, key responsibility areas, weaknesses, capabilities and where all they need his guidance and hand-holding. Calling employees by their first names not only motivates them to strive hard to deliver their level best but also leads to happy and satisfied employees. Organizations, where managers do not even know the names of their team members often face problems of high attrition rate, dissatisfied employees, conflicts and misunderstandings among employees eventually leading to lower productivity.

Let us go through certain things which are mandatory for a manager to know about his/her employees:

A manager needs to know the complete background of each and every individual who is a part of his team. Find out whether the individual concerned has:

- Any criminal record or not?
- How well has he/she performed in his previous organization?

- His/her credentials, past experience, specialization, interest levels and so on
- How frequently has he/she changed his/her previous organizations?
- His/her permanent residential address, contact numbers etc

Please do not forget to collect the photocopies of their educational certificates, passport or any other address verification proof for your own records. It helps you check the authenticity of an individual. You need to find out whether the other person is actually speaking the truth or not?

You really need to know individuals well before you recruit them in the team and make them responsible for ongoing projects. Reference checks are essential and help you in knowing a lot about an employee. Make sure, reference checks are done only when you are really sure of hiring the individual, else it might land the other person in trouble. Understand whether the individual really deserves to be a part of your team and organization or not? Do not hire individuals just because you have to fill a vacant position. Believe me, if you do not bother to know your employees well and verify their basic details, they would not stick around for a long time. Trust me, one fine day; they will disappear, leaving both you and your organization in deep trouble. You would have nothing to do if an employee leaves you in the middle of a project.

Managers ought to know the capabilities, expertise, skill sets of each and every individual. It helps in effective delegation of authority and tasks. Mismatch of job responsibilities leads to unnecessary confusions at the workplace. A manager needs to know interest areas and hobbies of employees to understand them better. As a manager, you need to know which employee can perform what all tasks with perfection and where all he /she still needs some improvement. You need to understand an employee's growth plan and his/her role in the team as well as organization. A manager ought to know what motivates an individual to perform as per expectations.

Managers need to know the contact numbers of all their team members. You need to know the birthdays and anniversaries of your employees. Do not forget to wish them on their special days for them to feel important at the workplace.

Role of Communication in Knowing Employees

It is essential for managers to know their employees well to expect loyalty and commitment in return. Employees need to feel comfortable at the workplace for them to deliver their level best. It is completely unprofessional to address your employees as "Mr","Ms"" or "hey". There is absolutely no need to address them as "Sir" or "Madam" even. It is absolutely okay if you call them by their first names.

Communication plays an important role in knowing your fellow workers. The role of a supervisor is not just to exchange mails with his team members. You need to sit with your employees and understand what exactly they expect from you and the organization. Find out whether they are satisfied with their performances or overall job responsibilities or not? You need to know where all he is lacking and what all initiatives would help him perform even better. Interaction is very important. Yes, emails are essential but why do you always have to depend on emails and SMSes? Why can't you directly speak to the individual concerned? Trust me, it will solve half of your problems and make work easier for you.

There is absolutely no harm if you speak to members of other departments as well. Sideways communication plays a crucial role in strengthening the bond among employees. Knowing employees well also enables managers to understand which employee can perform a particular task and which employee cannot? It helps you decide the key responsibility areas of your team members as per their specialization and capabilities. It is important for you to know whether an individual has any criminal background or not, how has he performed at his previous organization, his contact number, address and so on. If you do not keep a proper track on your employees, don't be surprised if he leaves the organization all of a sudden.

Interacting with employees does not mean you start interfering in someone's personal lives.

Informal interactions are also important to break the ice and know your employees. Encourage morning meetings at workplace where employees can plan their day and also brainstorm ideas to come up with innovative solutions. Trust me; it will increase the overall productivity of the employee as well as organization. Allow employees to bring their cups of coffee with them. Let them open up.

Greet everyone with a smile. No employee can work at a stretch for nine to ten hours. Encourage employees to have lunch together. Let employees interact with each other. Even managers can join their team members for lunch or small get-togethers once in a while. It is the responsibility of the human resource professionals to send birthday greetings to the employees.

Celebrate important festivals at workplace which would bring employees closer and also give them an opportunity to interact with each other. Such small initiatives also lead to a healthy work culture. No one likes to work in an organization where employees do not speak with each other.

Employees should have an easy access to their manager's cabin. Healthy Communication leads to free flow of information and better relationships at workplace.

How to Know Your Employees ?

Managers need to know their employees for them to feel valued and indispensable for the organization. Even the best of salaries and facilities would not help you retain your employees, if you do not appreciate and acknowledge their hard work. You need to know your employees' well - their capabilities, skill sets, expertise and also their weak spots, career goals, growth plans and so on. Find out what motivates them and what makes them unhappy.

Let us go through various ways which help managers know their team members.

Encourage healthy communication at workplace. Every employee irrespective of his /her designation and level in the hierarchy should have the liberty to express his/her views and opinions. Let individuals interact with each other and come up with their problems as well as innovative ideas which would not only increase their productivity but also benefit the organization. Managers need to communicate with the team members to make them feel comfortable and important at the workplace.

Interacting with employees will help you know many things about an individual which you would never come to know if you maintain a distance from him/her. If you do not speak to them, they would never come to you with their problems and eventually lose interest in work. Call employees together on a common platform to brainstorm ideas or discuss major issues.

Merely addressing a single individual every time might make the other team members feel ignored and left out. Office is not a place where you can favour someone just because he is your friend or relative. Managers ought to be approachable. It is essential to connect with your employees. Have lunch with them or go out for picnics or parties with your subordinates once in a while. Encourage employees to celebrate important festivals at workplace. Such activities bring individuals not only from a single team but all other departments closer to each other. Stand by your team and support them whenever they need your assistance. Once in a while, sit with them at their workstations and find out how they have planned their day or month, how would they achieve their targets, what all assistance they need from your end? and what all is going on in their personal lives?

Managers or team leaders should not only depend on human resource professionals to recruit new talent. Make sure to meet the new individual once before releasing the final offer letter. Do not ask your favourite employee to explain the new member his/her job responsibilities. Remember, as a manager, you are face of your team. Do make it a point to sit with the new member and induct him/her into the organization. Find out how the new employee can make a difference to your team and organization on the whole.

Employees expect your handholding and guidance always. Greet them with a smile. Wish them on their birthdays or anniversaries. Save their contact numbers and also put a reminder in your mobile so that you do not forget their special days. Believe me, a message from a manager to his team members will make their day even more special.

Review their work on a regular basis. It helps you know what employees are up to and in which all areas they need your guidance? Managers need to understand their team members beyond their work.

Role of Leadership in Knowing Employees

Employees are the backbone of an organization who play a crucial role in its success and failure. Employees need to feel comfortable at workplace and work should never be a mere source of burden for them. Employees ought to be valued if you want them to deliver their level best. They need to be appreciated and their hard work ought to be acknowledged in front of all.

Leadership plays a crucial role in knowing your employees.

Believe me, gone are the days when managers used to keep their subordinates at arm's length. This way, please do not expect your team members to listen to you or respect you. You need to make your employees feel important at workplace. Remember, as a manager, your job is not only to delegate responsibilities to your team members but also take them along. Please *do not restrict yourself to your cabins only*. Come out, sit with your team members, find out what they have planned for the entire day, know whether they are satisfied with their performance or not and so on.

What is the use of being a manager if you do not know what your team members are up to? Always make it a habit to call your team members by their first name. Avoid calling them by their nicknames. It is completely unprofessional. *Make it a point to speak to your team members at least once in a day. Enquire about their family members, their well being etc but do not interfere*

too much in their personal lives. They might not like it. Employees expect managers to enquire about their personal lives but you do not need to interfere much.

Join your team members for lunch once in a while. Be careful; do not discuss only work during lunch hours. If you do so, don't be surprised if your team members don't call you for lunch the next day. ***Take them out for small get-togethers after work***. Ask your employees to bring their families as well. As a manager, you have to take the initiative to bring the employees closer to each other and also know each other well.

Organize small activities at the workplace which help break the ice among employees. Who says you can't be friends with your co workers. Yes competition is necessary at workplace but do not forget that we need people around to speak to, discuss our problems, share our happiness and so on. After all, we are human beings, not machines. There is no problem if you speak to individuals representing other departments as long as you are not revealing your team's projects and strategies.

You need to be a strong leader who plays a crucial role in letting your team members know that there is someone who cares for them. They need to be supported and assisted in their day to day operations. Strong leadership goes a long way in binding the team together. Know what motivates your employees. Find out what all is lacking in your team members and what all additional skills can make them a better and efficient resource.

What is Employee Relations ?

An organization can't perform only with the help of chairs, tables, fans or other non living entities. It needs human beings who work together and perform to achieve the goals and objectives of the organization.

The human beings working together towards a common goal at a common place (organization) are called employees. Infact the employees are the major assets of an organization.

The success and failure of any organization is directly proportional to the labour put by each and every employee.

The employees must share a good rapport with each other and strive hard to realize the goal of the organization. They should complement each other and work together as a single unit. For the employees, the organization must come first and all their personal interests should take a back seat.

What is Employee Relations ?

Every individual shares a certain relationship with his colleagues at the workplace. The relationship is either warm, so-so or bad. The relationship can be between any one in the organization - between co workers, between an employee and his superior, between two members in the management and so on. It is important that the employees share a healthy relationship with each other to deliver their best performances.

An individual spends his maximum time at the workplace and his fellow workers are the ones with whom he spends the maximum hours in a day. No way can he afford to fight with his colleagues. Conflicts and misunderstandings only add to tensions and in turn decrease the productivity of the individual. One needs to discuss so many things at work and needs the advice and suggestions of all to reach to a solution which would benefit the individual as well as the organization.

No individual can work alone. He needs the support and guidance of his fellow workers to come out with a brilliant idea and deliver his level best.

Employee relations refer to the relationship shared among the employees in an organization. The employees must be comfortable with each other for a healthy environment at work. It is the prime duty of the superiors and team leaders to discourage conflicts in the team and encourage a healthy relationship among employees.

Life is really short and it is important that one enjoys each and every moment of it.Remember in an organization you are paid for your hard work and not for cribbing or fighting with each other. Don't assume that the person sitting next to you is your enemy or will do any harm to you. Who says you can't make friends at work, infact one can make the best of friends in the office. There is so much more to life than fighting with each other.

Observation says that a ***healthy relation among the employees goes a long way in motivating the employees and increasing their confidence and morale***. One starts enjoying his office and does not take his work as a burden. He feels charged and fresh the whole day and takes each day at work as a new challenge. If you have a good relation with your team members you feel going to office daily. Go out with your team members for a get together once in a while or have your lunch together. These activities help in strengthening the bond among the employees and improve the relations among them.

An employee must try his level best to adjust with each other and compromise to his best extent possible. If you do not agree to any of your fellow worker's ideas, there are several other ways to convince him. Sit with him and probably discuss with him where he is going wrong and needs a correction. This way he would definitely look up to you for your advice and guidance in future. He would trust you and would definitely come to your help whenever you need him. One should never spoil his relations with his colleagues because you never know when you need the other person.

Avoid using foul words or derogatory sentences against anyone. Don't depend on lose talk in office as it spoils the ambience of the place and also the relation among the employees. Blame games are a strict no no in office.

One needs to enter his office with a positive frame of mind and should not unnecessarily make issues out of small things. It is natural that every human being can not think the way you think, or behave the way you behave. If you also behave in the similar way the other person is behaving, there is hardly any difference between you and him. Counsel the other person and correct him wherever he is wrong.

It is of utmost importance that employees behave with each other in a cultured way, respect each other and learn to trust each other. An individual however hardworking he is, cannot do wonders alone. It is essential that all the employees share a cordial relation with each other, understand each other's needs and expectations and work together to accomplish the goals and targets of the organization.

Importance of Employee Relations - Why Employee Relations at Workplace?

Every individual at the workplace shares a certain relationship with his fellow workers. Human beings are not machines who can start working just at the push of a mere button. They need people to talk to, discuss ideas with each other and share their happiness and sorrows. An individual cannot work on his own, he needs people around. If the organization is all empty, you will not feel like sitting there and working. An isolated environment demotivates an individual and spreads negativity around. It is essential that people are comfortable with each other and work together as a single unit towards a common goal.

It is important that employees share a healthy relation

with each other at the work place. Let us find out why employee relations are important in an organization:

- *There are several issues on which an individual cannot take decisions alone*. He needs the guidance and advice of others as well. Sometimes we might miss out on important points, but our fellow workers may come out with a brilliant idea which would help us to achieve our targets at a much faster rate. Before implementing any plan, the pros and cons must be evaluated on an open forum where every employee has the right to express his opinions freely. On your own, you will never come to know where you are going wrong, you need people who can act as critic and correct you wherever you are wrong. If you do not enjoy a good relation with others no one will ever come to help you.

- *Work becomes easy if it is shared among all*. A healthy relation with your fellow workers would ease the work load on you and in turn increases your productivity. One cannot do everything on his own. Responsibilities must be divided among team members to accomplish the assigned tasks within the stipulated time frame. If you have a good rapport with your colleagues, he will always be eager to assist you in your assignments making your work easier.

- *The organization becomes a happy place to work if the employees work together as a family*. An individual tends to lose focus and concentration if his mind is always clouded with unnecessary tensions and stress. It has been observed that if people talk and discuss things with each other, tensions automatically evaporate and one feels better. Learn to trust others, you will feel relaxed. One doesn't feel like going to office if he is not in talking terms with the person sitting next to him. An individual spends around 8-9 hours in a day at his workplace and practically it is not possible that one works non stop without a break. You should have people with whom you can share your lunch, discuss movies or go out for a stroll once in a while. If you fight with everyone, no one will speak to you and you will be left all alone. It is important to respect others to expect the same from them.

- *An individual feels motivated in the company of others whom he can trust and fall back on whenever needed*. One feels secure and confident and thus delivers his best. It is okay if you share your secrets with your colleagues but you should know where to draw the line. A sense of trust is important.

- *Healthy employee relations also discourage conflicts and fights among individuals*. People tend to adjust more and stop finding faults in each other. Individuals don't waste their time in meaningless conflicts and disputes, rather concentrate on their work and strive hard to perform better. They start treating each other as friends and try their level best to compromise and make everyone happy.

- *A healthy employee relation reduces the problem of absenteeism at the work place*. Individuals are more serious towards their work and feel like coming to office daily. They do not take frequent leaves and start enjoying their work. Employees stop complaining against each other and give their best

- ***It is wise to share a warm relation with your fellow workers, because you never know when you need them***. You may need them any time. They would come to your help only when you are nice to them. You might need leaves for some personal reasons; you must have a trusted colleague who can handle the work on your behalf. Moreover healthy employee relations also spread positivity around.

It is essential that employees are comfortable with each other for better focus and concentration, lesser conflicts and increased productivity.

Strategies to Improve Employee Relations

For the organization to perform better it is important that the employees are comfortable with each other, share a good rapport and work in close coordination towards a common objective. People feel responsible and motivated to do good work and enjoy their work rather than taking it as a burden.

It is important that the management promotes healthy employee relations at workplace to extract the best out of each individual. Competition is essential but it should not promote negativity or any kind of enmity among the employees.

Let us go through some steps and strategies for a healthy employee relationship in the organization.

- *Involve your team members:* They should feel important and indispensable for the organization. An individual must be assigned responsibilities according to their interests and responsibilities. Don't impose work on them. Let them willingly accept challenges. They must enjoy whatever they do otherwise they would end up fighting with their superiors and fellow workers.

- *Encourage individuals to share their work with each other:* This way people tend to talk with each other more, discuss things among themselves and thus the comfort level increases. Let them work together and take decisions on their own. A team leader should intervene only in extreme cases of conflicts and severe misunderstandings.

. *Assign them targets and ask all your team members to contribute equally and achieve the target within the desired time frame*. Motivate them to work in groups. This way employees have no other choice than to trust their fellow workers and take each other's help as well. An employee must have the liberty to express his ideas and all of them should sit together to decide on something which would be beneficial to all.

. *One should try his level best that all the employees must have their lunch together at the same time*. Half an hour to fourty five minutes must be dedicated to lunch and one should not discuss work during lunch time. There are other topics as well. Discuss movies, sports, shopping or any other thing under the sun. There will be no harm if the employees go out together once in a while for get togethers, picnics or shopping. Ask them to bring their family members as well.

- *Encourage effective communication among the team members*. It has been observed that poor communication leads to confusions and misunderstandings. The communication has to be precise and relevant. One should not play with words and be very specific about his expectations from his fellow workers as well as the organization. If you are not very happy with your colleague's proposal, don't keep things to yourself. Voice your opinion and do express your displeasure. It will definitely prevent a conflict among employees later and improve the relations among them. Be straightforward. Don't pretend things just to please your boss. If you find anything unacceptable, discuss with your superior but in a polite way.

- *Written modes of communication must be promoted among the employees for better transparency*. Verbal communication is not as reliable as written communication. The agendas, minutes of the meeting, important issues must be circulated among all through emails. Make sure that all the related employees are in the loop. Don't communicate individually with any of the employees as the other one might feel neglected and left out.

- *Morning meeting is another effective way to improve the relation among the employees*. Let everyone come together on a common platform and discuss whatever issues they have. The meetings must not be too formal. Allow the team members to bring their cups of coffee. Start your day with a positive mind. Greet everyone with a warm smile. Exchange greetings and compliments. If any of your team member is not in a pleasant mood, do take the initiative and ask what is wrong with him. Try your level best to provide him a solution.

- *Organize birthday parties, Christmas parties, New Year parties etc*. at the workplace. These small initiatives actually go a long way in strengthening the bond among the employees. Ask all of them to decorate the office, their work stations and make all the necessary arrangements themselves. You will actually be surprised to find out that everyone would be ready with some thing or the other. Employees would actually take the initiative and organize things on their own. Let them enjoy with each other and have fun.

Praise the individual if he has done something exceptionally well. Reward him suitably. The names of the top performers must be displayed on the notice boards for others to draw inspiration from them. Encourage everyone to perform well to live up to the expectations of the superiors as well as the management.

A healthy relation among employees promotes a positive ambience at the work place and employees feel happy and satisfied at work. They look forward to going to office daily and also work hard to realize their team's as well as organization's goals.

Employee Relationship Management

Employees are the major assets of an organization. It is essential that the employees perform together as a collective unit and contribute equally towards the realization of a common goal. No task can be accomplished if the individuals are engaged in constant conflicts and misunderstandings. It has been observed that targets are achieved at a much faster rate if the employees work together and share a warm relationship with each other. Employees must be comfortable with each other to deliver their best and enjoy their work.

What is employee relationship management ?

Employee relationship management refers to managing the relation between the various employees in an organization. The relationship can be between employee and the employer as well as between employees at the same level.

What is Management ?

Management is nothing but a technique which brings people together on a common platform and guides them so that they achieve their desired targets without fighting with each other. In a layman's language, management is nothing but managing things effectively so that tasks are accomplished without any hassles and confusions. Management is required everywhere.

Every individual goes for shopping. The moment you enter in an outlet, a sales person would come to you and assist you in your shopping. He would try his level best to convince you and guide you in selecting an outfit according to your taste as well as budget. The moment you finalize something, you automatically would be directed to the billing section for the monetary transactions. Your shopping basket in no time would reach the packing area where the officials would nicely put the outfits in a smart carry bag flaunting the logo of the store. Finally there would be a supervisor who would recheck your bill and thank you for your valuable time.

How do you think such a smooth coordination is possible? Not a single moment, there was any confusion. All this is possible through management. Every thing was well managed and organized effectively to avoid confusions and meet the ultimate objective of the store ie selling the product as well as making the customer happy.

Employee relationship management is an art which effectively monitors and manages the relation between individuals either of the same team or from different teams. Employee relationship management activity helps in strengthening the bond among the employees and ensures that each one is contented and enjoys a healthy relation with each other.

Employee relationship management includes various activities undertaken by the superiors or the management to develop a healthy relation among the employees and extract the best out of each team member.

Let us go through certain activities which are imperative for a healthy employee relationship management:

- *Transparency in communication is of utmost importance for a healthy employee relationship management*. A single point of contact must be assigned who should be made responsible for handling queries of all the team members and escalating it to the seniors. Confusions are bound to arise if all of them would walk up to their superiors with their problems. Let the team members decide their SPOC. In such cases employees actually know who to get in touch with in case of a query and in the absence of their superiors. The hierarchy should not be too complicated and every employee should be accessible to each other. Important information must be passed on in the presence of all, where everyone has the liberty to express his opinions freely. Important information can also be put on the notice boards for everyone to read and get a common picture. If any one has performed exceptionally well, do display his name on the bulletin board. Let everyone read it and get inspired to perform better next time. Encourage morning meetings where individuals can come together and know each other well. Exchanging information through emails is also an important way to improve the relation among the employees as everyone knows what is being communicated to the other individual.

- ***Encourage group activities at the workplace***. Motivate individuals to work together probably in a group so that the comfort level increases. The more they talk, the more they get to know each other. Give them a target, a deadline and ask them to take each other's help and reach to a conclusion. They would definitely come closer this way and start trusting each other more.

An individual spends the maximum time at his workplace and one should treat his team members as a part of one's extended family. It is important to celebrate festivals at organization, the same way we do at our homes. Celebrate each other's birthday and do ask for treats. Such informal get togethers go a long way in improving the relation among the employees. Individuals come together, enjoy together and come to know lot many things which actually they don't bother to find out during the normal working hours. Families must also be invited for a better bonding. The team leaders must ask their team members to take their lunch together so that they discuss other things apart from their daily work.

- *Assign challenging work to your team members so that they feel motivated to deliver their level best*. Do not assign something which they do not find interesting. The responsibilities must be divided equally among the team members and no employee should be overburdened. Every employee should be aware of his key responsibility areas to avoid confusions. No way should the work get monotonous.

- *The concept of workstations and cubicles must be promoted rather than closed cabins*. People sitting in closed cabins tend to get cut off from rest of the employees in the organization and are generally lost in their own sweet world. They would enter their cabins in the morning and come out in the evening and thus sometimes even don't get the opportunity to exchange greetings with their fellow workers. People sitting in workstations tend to talk to each other more often even in between work and thus relationship improves. One can even walk up to the other's desk to have a brief chit chat in order to take a small break and feel relaxed. Employees sitting together discuss many things and even share their secrets, thus the trust increases. It is commonly observed that if any of your colleagues sitting next to you is on leave for some days, you start missing him.

- ***The employees must be motivated to avoid politics and blame games at work***. Such activities are considered highly unproductive and spoil the relationship among the employees. Backbiting is a strict no no at the workplace. Avoid getting into unnecessary controversies and useless criticism at work. Respect your team members as well as your superiors. It is important that one trusts his management rather than unnecessarily cribbing and finding faults. Avoid conflicts and try to adjust with each other. It is okay to be friends with your colleagues but don't have unrealistic expectations from anyone.

Last but not the least ***the superiors or the team leaders must not act pricy and try to dominate their team members***. The "Hitler approach" does not work now a days. No one should be afraid of his boss, instead treat him as his well-wisher and mentor who is always there to support him. The employees must be able to fall back on their team leader anytime. The team leader must understand the needs and expectations of his employees and should not be too harsh to them. If they want a leave for a genuine reason, do grant them. Don't be after their life if you find them chatting with their family or friends over the phone once in a while or log on to any social networking site. These things are natural but make sure the work does not suffer.

- ***Partialities must be avoided for a better employee relationship***. Treat everyone as one and every individual must respect each other's privacy. There is a limit to everything and thus over indulgence in each other's work, too much of a friendly nature should be avoided.

For a better employee relationship management, it is important that employees have a positive frame of mind and don't always consider their colleagues as their enemies. Don't always assume that your fellow team member would say something against you in front of your boss. Avoid disputes, misunderstandings, instead work together, enjoy together and make the organization a better place to work.

Role of Communication in Employee Relationship

A healthy employee relationship ensures a positive environment at work and also helps the employees to achieve their targets at a much faster rate. People are more focussed, can concentrate better in their assignments and hence the output increases. Employees are not engaged in constant fights, are eager to help each other and do not take work as a burden. They enjoy each and every moment at work and do not take leaves often.

Communication is not only important in our daily lives but also plays a crucial role at workplace. It is one of the most important factors which either improves or spoils the relationship among employees.

The communication has to be transparent and precise for a warm relationship among employees. Clarity in thoughts is important. Don't assume that the other person will come to know on his own what is going on in your mind. The thoughts must be converted sensibly into relevant words such that the other person is able to understand you well.

The employees must be very clear about what is being expected from them. Their key responsibility areas, roles and responsibilities must be communicated to them in the desired form for them to perform their level best. Don't play with words. Be straightforward and precise in what you expect from your team members. Don't blame them later. Haphazard thoughts and abstract ideas only lead to confusions and spoil the relationship among the employees.

Let us go through the below example:

Janet was working as a key accounts manager with a leading advertising firm. First she wanted Ted to prepare a report on marketing and sales strategies undertaken by her organization, then she wanted him to prepare a report on the branding techniques and finally she asked him to also include the promotion strategies. She herself was not very clear about her expectations. Poor Ted was so confused that he submitted an incomplete report to Janet. She was not at all happy with Ted's performance and always side-lined him in future.

In the above example, Janet was not very clear about the content of the report and also confused Ted. One needs to express his ideas clearly for the other person to understand it correctly. Poor communication in this case spoiled the relation between Janet and Ted who were once good friends.

Had Janet told Ted to prepare an exhaustive report on Marketing, sales, branding as well as the promotion techniques undertaken by the organization, things would been crystal clear and Ted would not have made any mistakes. One should be first very clear about his needs, expectations and then only communicate it to the other person.

Don't change statements quite often. Be firm. One should not tamper any data or manipulate truth. You would never gain anything out of it. Be honest and pass on information in its desired form. If your boss has asked you to download some information to your fellow team members, please do pass it on as it is. Don't try to add or delete words as it would earn you a bad name. No one would trust you in future or come to your help whenever required. Remember honesty always pays in the long run.

Think twice before you speak. Avoid using foul words against anyone at the workplace as it spoils the ambience of the office and leads to several disputes among individuals*.* Don't say anything which would hurt anyone. Avoid lose talks. It is okay to enjoy at work but one should never cross his limit. If you do not agree to anyone's ideas, it is better to discuss things with him rather being rude or harsh. Whatever you communicate has to be crisp, relevant and should make sense. Don't utter non sense at work. Be a little professional in your approach.

Important information should be passed on in the presence of each and every employee for better clarity*.*

Every employee should have the liberty to express his views and ideas. Don't expect you would clear your doubts later on, ask questions then and there. No one would feel bad, rather appreciate your interest and attentiveness but do not jump in between. Do wait for your turn to speak. Don't meet anyone separately as the other person might feel neglected or left out resulting in major displeasure and conflict among the team members. Do take care of your pitch and tone. It should not be too loud.

Depend more on written modes of communication as they are more reliable as compared to verbal communication. An individual might back out if the information is passed on to him verbally as there are no records, but it never happens in written modes of communication. Prefer passing on information through Emails. All the related team members must be marked a carbon copy so that everyone knows what is being communicated to his fellow member. One should master the art of writing emails. Remember an email is nothing but a mirror image of one's thoughts. Make sure that your mail is self-explanatory and everyone is clear about your ideas and opinions.

An employee needs to be constantly motivated to avoid a dip in his performance. If someone has performed exceptionally well, do not hesitate to praise him. Words like "Well done","Bravo","Great Performance" go a long way in making the individual happy. If you are satisfied with your team member's performance, do communicate your feelings to him.

Communicate effectively with your fellow team members and you would never have a problem with anyone. People would respect you and work would be fun for you.

Role of Motivation in Employee Relationship

A healthy employee relationship leads to an increased level of satisfaction among the employees and in turn an increased productivity. Workplace becomes a much happier place and employees tend to concentrate more on work rather than unproductive things.

Motivation plays an important role in a healthy employee relationship.

A motivated employee works better and at a much faster rate as compared to others. Motivating the employee would in turn benefit the organization only. You need to charge your cell phone after sometime for it to operate well, similarly a human being needs to be motivated from time to time to avoid a dip in his performance and for him to remain loyal towards the management. Motivation acts as a catalyst for organization's success and helps the individuals to remain productive and deliver better results everytime.

Simple words like "Well done", "Bravo", "Great", "Wow" can actually work wonders and go a long way in motivating an individual. If any employee has done exceptionally well, do appreciate him. Give him a pat on his back. The employees feel contended at work and thus share a warm relationship with their superiors. They do not badmouth anyone in the office or speak ill of their organization. Higher motivation rate results in more satisfied employees. Every organization invests time and money to groom an individual and make him a corporate material. It is absolutely an organization's loss if it is not able to retain its employees. A motivated employee would stick to an organization for a longer duration and enjoy a healthy relationship with his colleagues and fellow workers. He would not be engaged in disputes and instead work hard to achieve his targets and in a way benefitting the organization.

A token of appreciation is a must. Cash prize, gift vouchers and shopping coupons help in motivating the employees to a great extent. Every individual tries hard to win the prize money and does not get time to fight or criticize others. They do not lose focus and instead take each other's help to accomplish their tasks within the stipulated time frame. They get a motive to work.

The employees must be motivated not to spread negativity around. They should be encouraged not to make issues out of small things and do not bring their personal tensions to work. They should be made to realize the importance of team work at the workplace and healthy relation with colleagues. No one should forget their purpose of coming to the organization.

Motivate employees to work in a group rather than working alone. They must realize that working in a group means a better exchange of ideas and thoughts to come to an unique idea fruitful for them as well as the organization. Employees should be motivated to help each other and treat their team members as a part of their extended family. Individuals should complement each other at work but one should not forget his limit. Too much of a friendly nature again leads to problems and unrealistic expectations.

Award ceremonies must be organized at the workplace every month or after every three months to acknowledge the top performers. Call them on the dais and honour them. Display their names on the company's main notice board so that every employee gets to know about it. Give the top performers badges for them to flaunt and do this activity in the presence of all. Don't do it separately as the other employee might get hurt and start fighting with his team members. These kinds of activities slightly give an upper edge to the employees who have worked hard and performed well. Others also feel inspired to perform better next time.

Job rotations and promotions are also an important way to motivate the employees. The management must ensure that each one is happy with their work and monotony does not creep in to the team. When an individual does not enjoy his work, he would always look for excuses to fight with his colleagues and spoil the environment. He would be indulged in lose talks and always blame others for his non performance leading to an unhealthy relation among employees.

It is important that the employees are motivated well to extract the best out of them and ensure a healthy relation among the employees.

Role of Attitude in Employee Relationship

The performance of an individual is largely dependent on the relation he shares with his colleagues. It is really important that individuals are friendly with their colleagues so that they can discuss several issues with each other and come to a conclusion best suited to all. No individual can perform alone. Tasks are accomplished at a much faster rate when the work load is shared among all and each one contributes in his best possible way. Nothing productive has ever come out of conflicts and disputes. They in turn lead to major rifts among employees and create stress at the workplace. Why to unnecessarily spoil relations with people? You never know when you might need the other person.

Attitude plays an important role in improving the relationship among the individuals. Nothing is possible unless and until an individual has a positive attitude towards life. You might have excellent communication skills, might be an intelligent worker, but if you don't have a positive attitude; you would definitely fail to create an impression of yours. People would be reluctant to speak to you and you would be left all alone.

An individual should never ever have a negative attitude at workplace. It is dangerous. Your organization pays you and in turn expects quality work from you, so why unnecessarily crib over things. It is always better to accept things with a smiling face. If your boss assigns you some task, it means that he finds you capable enough to handle the assignment. Consider yourself fortunate and the chosen one. Don't make faces as your superior might feel bad and eventually lose his trust on you. Clear all your doubts with the person, who has delegated you the responsibility, rather than criticising and making fun in front of others who are not involved.

Don't always find faults in others. No two individuals are alike. The other person might not be as intelligent or as educated as you are, try your level best to adjust with him. Adjustment does not mean accepting any wrong things, rather it is compromising sometimes.

Sam and Sara were team members and sat at adjacent workstations. Sam had a habit of constantly chatting over the phone with his friends and family, which sometimes irritated Sara.

Case - 1 Sara always thought that Sam did it intentionally to disturb her. She fought with Sam terribly and now has strained relationship with her team member.

Case - 2 Sara spoke to Sam about her displeasure, convinced him and requested him to either speak a little low or go outside for attending calls. Now a days Sara and Sam are best of friends and together they contribute effectively to their team's targets.

Case 2 is any day a far better option.

One should not be too rigid or adamant. Be a little more flexible. Don't always assume that the other person is wrong and only you are correct. You may be wrong sometimes. Listen to what the other person has to say and then only come to a conclusion. Don't take any decisions with a blocked mind.

An individual should not make issues out of small things. It is always better to forget things. Ignore things as long as they are not affecting your team's performance. Don't take things to heart. The more you become negative for your colleagues, the more you fight with them and in turn spoil your relationship.

One should be forgiving. If your boss is angry with you over something, do take the initiative and say a sorry to him. A simple "Sorry" can actually do wonders. If you do not have the courage to talk to him, send him a sms. Saying sorry will not lower your self-esteem, instead it would strengthen the bond between you and your superior.

One should never backstab anyone just for the sake of a mere promotion or some money. It is unethical. Human relationships are more important and should be valued.

Don't carry your ego to work. Everyone is equal at workplace. Respect one and all as everyone is an employee just like you. Don't treat anyone as untouchables.

One should always keep his personal life separate from his professional affairs. Don't drag your personal tensions to work. Try to keep a balance between the two. You cannot afford to ill-treat your colleague just because you had a fight with your spouse the previous night. Your fellow team members have nothing to do with it. Learn to enjoy life. One should always look at the brighter side of life.

Treat your colleagues as your friends. Give them time and try to mingle with them as much as you can. Go out together for shopping or for a movie once in a while. You will feel attached to them. The trust factor and the comfort level increases.

Remember there is always some light at the end of a dark tunnel. Never lose hope in life. Stay positive, be good to others and enjoy a healthy relation with one and all.

Role of HR in Employee Relationship

It is rightly said that the success and failure of an organization is directly proportional to the relationship shared among the employees. The employees must share a cordial relation otherwise they would always end up fighting with each other. Nothing is possible without trust.

You need to trust people to expect the best out of them. Trust only comes when you are comfortable with the other person. An individual can't always take decisions alone. Employees together can discuss things among themselves, come out with innovative ideas and accomplish the tasks at a much faster rate.

A human resource professional plays a key role in binding the employees together. He/she must undertake certain activities which help in strengthening the bond among the employees and bring them closer.

The individual taking care of the HR activities plays a key role in involving all the employees into something productive which would give them an opportunity to know each other well. Individuals are so engrossed in their daily routine work that they hardly get time to interact with each other. Many of them don't even know the full names of the person sitting next to their workstations. The human resource department must ensure that several group activities are being organized at the workplace to bring all employees on a common platform.

Research says that if the employees are satisfied with their job responsibilities, they tend to remain happy and avoid conflicts with each other. Individuals develop a feeling of trust and loyalty towards their organization and don't waste their time and energy in unproductive tasks.

Organize various activities like potlucks and small get togethers at the workplace. Ask each one to bring some dish according to his taste and convenience. Let the employees enjoy together. Employees tend to discuss lot many things apart from routine work in these kinds of informal get togethers.

One day probably the last day of the month should be earmarked with the sole objective of celebrating birthdays falling in the particular month. For example all those born in the month of May should celebrate their birthdays together on the last day of the month i.e. 31st May which will help a great deal for them to remain charged for next one year. The HR should send a formal mail inviting all. Let everyone enjoy and have fun. Divide individuals into groups and ask each group to do something. One group can probably be responsible for the decoration of the venue; the other group can take care of the cake as well as other eatables and so on. The HR person should ideally support each group to ensure that no one faces any difficulty in getting things organized.

It is the responsibility of the human resources team to organize various events like sports day, annual day, green day etc. ***The employees must be encouraged to participate in these kinds of extra curricular activities***. Employees are able to relax this way and take a break from their routine work. Problems crop up when the work tends to become monotonous. Employees should enjoy coming to office, rather than treating work as a burden.

The HR in coordination with the team leaders must display the names of the top performers every month on the company's noticeboard.Send a congratulations mail as well. The human resource professional along with the supervisor can even hand over a small trophy as a token of appreciation to the top performers. Do this activity in the presence of all. The one who has performed well starts trusting his management more and strives hard to win many more trophies in the future. Everyone is aware about each other's performance and gets inspired as well.

While making the organization's policies, the human resource department must fix a common time for lunch for all the employees. *Assign half an hour for the same and make sure that no one during the lunch time is seen working at their workstations*. Everyone should come together at the office canteen and take lunch together. When people sit together, half of their problems disappear on their own. Employees share their sorrows, displeasures and various other problems with their colleagues and this way come closer to each other. People develop better bonding this way.

When a new employee joins an organization, make sure he receives a warm welcome by all. The induction program should be conducted at the auditorium or the conference room so that everyone can be invited. Ask the new joinee to introduce himself well. Let others know that a new member has stepped into their family to help them in their assignments.

The HR along with the line managers must communicate the key responsibility areas clearly to the employees to extract the best out of them and avoid dissatisfactions later.

Employee Satisfaction and Need of Employee Satisfaction

In today's scenario where there is no dearth of competitors in the market, it is essential that employees work with dedication and sincerity. How do you expect a new joinee to develop a sense of loyalty and attachment towards the organization all of a sudden? The poor fellow does not know much about your company and it does take time for everyone to adjust in the system. Respect towards the organization comes with due course of time only when the employee is treated well by his superiors.

Employee satisfaction is a state where individuals are not only happy with their current profiles but also look forward towards a long term association with the organization. No individual wants to quit his/her job after every six months. But the moment monotony creeps in, people start looking for better opportunities. Most of the times, employees treat their jobs just as a mere source of earning their bread and butter. They come to office not because they enjoy their work but because they need their salaries to ensure a comfortable living.

Employees would never be satisfied with their jobs unless and until they have something interesting and challenging to work on. "Monday morning blues" is a common term used by professionals as an excuse for not coming to work and feeling lazy on the first day of the week. I personally do not agree with this. Trust me, if you really enjoy your work, you would feel like coming to office every day. Do we ever crib when we have a holiday or are at home? NO. Why? Just because we feel comfortable at our home. Why do we then always complain at work? Understand, there is a difference between your personal and professional life. Think logically. The moment you have unrealistic expectations at workplace, problems are bound to arise and you can never be happy and contended at workplace.

Both management and employees have an important role to play in ensuring a positive ambience at the workplace and eventually job satisfaction. Employees should not be created as mere robots that simply start working just at the click of a button and neither express themselves nor create problems for others. Management needs to stand by their employees and constantly mentor them. Employees are indispensable for the organization but in no way, pride and ego should get into their heads. Do not be under the impression that superiors would treat you with respect even if you do not perform. Such a thing is practically impossible in the professional scenario. Be positive and learn to adjust. Try to be happy and satisfied with what all you have got rather than cribbing over small issues.

It is crucial for the employees to be satisfied with their jobs, else neither they would be able to deliver as per expectations nor feel comfortable at the workplace. Believe me; satisfaction is all in our minds. Sometimes, we are satisfied with small things also and sometimes we find a problem even in the best of situations. How many jobs would you change? Believe me, there is a problem everywhere, only the nature of problem would vary. The idea is not to run away from problems but face them with a smile. Satisfied employees willingly work towards the fulfilment of organization's goals and objectives, eventually assuring profits and higher revenues. Unsatisfied employees often badmouth their organization which has a serious impact on the image of the particular brand. Employees who are satisfied with their jobs stick around for a long time, benefitting the organization with their expertise and experience.

Ways to Improve Employee Satisfaction

Employee satisfaction plays an essential role in motivating the employees to deliver their level best and also leads to a positive ambience at the workplace.

Employee satisfaction is no rocket science and trust me; it does not take much to satisfy your employees. Small but sincere efforts are enough to satisfy employees so that they not only enjoy their current roles and responsibilities but also stick to the organization for a long time.

Let us go through ways which improve employee satisfaction.

Individuals should be assigned work as per their expertise, interest area and specialization. If you expect a marketing guy to do justice in an accounts profile, he is bound to get demotivated, which would eventually affect his performance. Discuss with the employees at the time of their joining only as to what profile would suit them the most to avoid confusions later on. Key responsibility areas should be communicated to the employees very clearly from day one. If employees work on something which they are best at, not only they would be happy and satisfied but also yield better results.

No employee should be overburdened. Work has to be equally distributed among all. Why should only one employee do everything while others just come, enjoy and go back home? Favouritsm and partialities have no place in the professional world. Please do not give less work to someone just because he is your friend and you like him. This way, others who actually end up doing more work eventually lose interest and start looking for better opportunities.

Promote a healthy work culture. ***Encourage employees to talk to each other, discuss among themselves and work as a single unit not for themselves but for the organization.*** It is indeed the responsibility of the management to make their employees realize that they all are a part of a single family and it is foolish to fight amongst themselves and create unnecessary problems for each other. Let them have their lunch together or go out for small get togethers once in a while. This way, they seldom find office monotonous, are satisfied with their jobs and also work with full dedication.

Employees are unsatisfied the most when their voices are not heard. It might be a small problem for you but for the other person, it can be a major cause of concern. Grievances need to be addressed on an immediate basis. It is the responsibility of the human resource professionals to sit with their employees on a regular basis and find out whether they are satisfied with their jobs or not? Let them come out with their problems.

Give ample growth opportunities to employees. Employees lose interest in work, the moment they have nothing new to do. Give them new assignements, new challenges, new roles so that they get to learn something interesting every day. Do not unnecessarily pressurize them for unrealistic targets. Do not interfere much and let them work in their own way. Guide them whenever required.

Not appreciating the employees when they have performed well leads to dissatisfaction and negativity in them. The credit should not always go to the top management and team leaders but to the employees as well.

Bosses should not forget that their role is not to shout on their subordinates but to handhold them and stand by them even in the worst situations. Majority of the employees are frustrated because they do not have an understanding BOSS.

Nothing works better than rewarding employees suitably and releasing their salaries on time. Most of the times, employees have a problem because they do not get their incentives and payments when they require the most. Why would an individual slog for an entire day if he does not require money? Do not create too much of a problem in clearing their bills.

Do not exploit them. Treat them with utmost respect and care.

Role of Communication in Employee Satisfaction

Employee satisfaction is of utmost importance for organizations to grow and also survive the cut throat competition. Remember, employees are your true assets and it is essential that they remain happy and satisfied with their jobs for them to strive hard and deliver their level best.

Communication plays a crucial role in employee satisfaction.

Most of the problems arise when employees are not happy with their bosses. On top of it, rather than discussing the issue face to face with their immediate reporting bosses, they prefer to badmouth them behind their backs. Understand that this is not the solution. Bosses need to realize one thing that there are very few individuals who really have the courage to come up with their grievances in front of their superiors. For them, the easiest solution is to sit quietly and do nothing or simply look for another job. You need to motivate your employees to open up in front of you. You need to make the employees feel that you are always there with him irrespective of the circumstances and situations.

Communicate with your team members effectively. Sit with them, talk to them and find out what extra you can do for them to ensure hundred percent dedication and cooperation from their end. Do not allow the employees to keep everything within themselves. Employees are the most satisfied when they share a great rapport with their bosses. Communicating with them on a regular basis helps you know whether they are really happy with their jobs or not. If they are enjoying their work, you are doing a good work and if they are not, you really should look into the matter on an urgent basis if you really want to retain your employee.

Do an exercise tomorrow and you will find an answer yourself as to why communication is so important.

For two days, do not speak to anyone and work in isolation. Trust me, at the end of the day, you will not feel like coming back to work again. That is the power of communication. Work would become a burden for employees if you do not allow them to interact with each other. Not only the employees would be frustrated but also develop a feeling of hatred towards superiors as well as their organization. Let employees talk to each other and sort out problems among themselves.

Employees are dissatisfied when information does not reach them correctly. Make them a part of important discussions where they can also share their ideas and opinions. Healthy communication ensures accurate information reaches all employees and no one feels left out within the system. Do not set targets for your team members unless and until you discuss with them. How can you set goals for your team without knowing whether your team is really capable of achieving targets within the stipulated time frame or not? If you decide the job responsibilities of an individual on his/her behalf; very soon, he would be frustrated and decide to move on. Appraisals and promotions need to be discussed in the presence of employees. Trust me, if you do so, employees would work because they want to take their organization to a new level and not because their Bosses have asked them to do so.

Healthy work culture leads to satisfied employees who not only deliver their level best but also stick around for a long time. Half of the problems evaporate if discussed. Effective communication also goes a long way in reducing negativity at the workplace which eventually leads to satisfied and happy employees. Won't you feel good if your boss walks up to your cubicle, gives a pat on your back and praises you for your performance in front of others? Would you ever think of quitting your job? I don't think so.

Importance of Employee Satisfaction

Employee satisfaction is of utmost importance for employees to remain happy and also deliver their level best. Satisfied employees are the ones who are extremely loyal towards their organization and stick to it even in the worst scenario. They do not work out of any compulsion but because they dream of taking their organization to a new level. Employees need to be passionate towards their work and passion comes only when employees are satisfied with their job and organization on the whole. Employee satisfaction leads to a positive ambience at the workplace. People seldom crib or complain and concentrate more on their work.

The first benefit of employee satisfaction is that individuals hardly think of leaving their current jobs. Employee satisfaction in a way is essential for employee retention. Organizations need to retain deserving and talented employees for long term growth and guaranteed success. If people just leave you after being trained, trust me, your organization would be in a big mess. Agreed you can hire new individuals but no one can deny the importance of experienced professionals. It is essential for organizations to have experienced people around who can guide freshers or individuals who have just joined.

Employee attrition is one of the major problems faced by organizations. I don't think an individual who is treated well at the workplace, has ample opportunities to grow, is appreciated by his superiors, gets his salary on time ever thinks of changing his job. Retaining talented employees definitely gives your organization an edge over your competitors as they contribute more effectively than new joinees. Moreover, no new individual likes to join an organization which has a high employee attrition rate. Employees who are not satisfied with their jobs often badmouth their organization and also warn friends and acquaintances to join the same.

Employee satisfaction is essential to ensure higher revenues for the organization. No amount of trainings or motivation would help, unless and until individuals develop a feeling of attachment and loyalty towards their organization. Employees waste half of their time fighting with their counter parts or sorting out issues with them. Trust me; employees who are satisfied with their jobs seldom have the time to indulge in nasty office politics. They tend to ignore things and do not even have the time to crib or fight with others. Satisfied employees are the happy employees who willingly help their fellow workers and cooperate with the organization even during emergency situations. Such employees do not think of leaving their jobs during crisis but work hard together as a single unit to overcome challenges and come out of the situation as soon as possible. For them, their organization comes first, everything else later. They do not come to office just for money but because they really feel for the organization and believe in its goals and objectives. Satisfied employees also spread positive word of mouth and always stand by each other. Instead of wasting their time in gossiping and loitering around they believe in doing productive work eventually benefitting the organization. They take pride in representing their respective organizations and work hard to ensure higher revenues for the organization.

Satisfied employees tend to adjust more and handle pressure with ease as compared to frustrated ones. Employees who are not satisfied with their jobs would find a problem in every small thing and be too rigid. They find it extremely difficult to compromise or cope up with the changing times. On the other hand, employees who are happy with their jobs willing participate in training programs and are eager to learn new technologies, softwares which would eventually help them in their professional career. Satisfied employees accept challenges with a big smile and deliver even in the worst of circumstances.

Factors Influencing Employee Satisfaction

Employee satisfaction ensures employees are happy with their jobs and also give their heart and soul to the organization. Such people seldom think of changing their jobs and motivate not only themselves but also others to work hard for the betterment of the organization.

Let us go through few factors influencing employee satisfaction:

Working conditions of an organization play an important role in influencing employee satisfaction. Employees who do not have a proper workstation and are not comfortable at their workplaces are the ones who are the most frustrated and unhappy with their job. Appoint people who are responsible for the cleanliness of the office and most importantly the rest rooms. Assign drawers and proper space to employees where they can keep their important documents, files and also personal belongings. Encourage the employees to keep their drawers and desk clean. Make sure your office building is fire resistant.

Management has no right to treat its employees as slaves just because they are being paid. Employees need to be treated with utmost respect and care. They need to feel protected at the workplace for them to develop a feeling of job satisfaction. Encourage healthy ambience at the workplace and also motivate employees not to participate in nasty office politics.

The second most important factor influencing employee satisfaction is employee benefits. Employees need to be paid well as per their designation and roles and responsibilities in the organization. The moment an employee is underpaid, he/she would create problems for the entire organization. Do not favour any employee. Make sure incentives and monetary benefits are directly proportional to the efforts an individual puts in. Do not unnecessary hold their payments and salaries if you want your employees to stick around for a long time.

Another reason as to why employees are not satisfied with their job is that their hard work is not acknowledged. Give them their due credit. If they have performed something extraordinarily, do not forget to appreciate them in front of their colleagues. Give them additional responsibilities. Give them an opportunity to handle teams. You need to trust them and guide them accordingly. If you expect an individual to work on entry level projects for next five years, you are sadly mistaken. He/she would definitely move on. Make sure deserving employees get decent hikes and benefits. Do not put a full stop on their career growth citing lame excuses that the individual concerned is not performing up to the mark or the organization is at loss. If the employee is not performing well then what is the management doing? In such a case he should not be in the system and if at all, he is there, what are seniors doing to improve his performance? Be transparent with your employees. An employee becomes frustrated the moment he has nothing challenging to work on. Constant upgradation of skills is essential for every employee to survive the cut throat competition. Make sure employees are a part of regular training programs.

Make employees feel as an indispensable resource for the organization. A sense of loyalty towards the organization does not come out of compulsion. It has to come from within. Give employees space and freedom to take their own decisions. If they have to depend on you for every small thing, trust me they would soon end up quitting their jobs. Give them the budget and ask them to perform and deliver within the stipulated time frame. Do not interfere in their way of handling teams.

Be reasonable with your employees. Trust me; being too strict with them does not help. If you expect them to work on every Sunday, do not be surprised if they resign all of a sudden.

Role of Employees to Ensure Job Satisfaction

You may have the best of office, best of infrastructure, in fact the best of everything but if you have the habit of finding faults and cribbing, you will always remain stressed out and frustrated. A lot depends on the employees as well. Remember, one needs to learn to see the positive sides of life.

Let us go through few tips which would ensure job satisfaction for employees.

Do not attend office just for the sake of earning money. Yes, money is one of the most important deciding factors as to why we all work so hard but remember, it is not everything. Trust me, if you work just for your salaries, you will never ever be satisfied with your job. Do not join an organization just because it is paying you well. Make sure you are aware of your key responsibility areas and your role in the organization is as per your knowledge and specialization and you already have some experience working on the same profile. If a finance professional accepts a marketing job just because he would get to earn huge incentives, he is bound to end up in a mess as it is not where his/her expertise lies. He would never find his job interesting and eventually lose interest in work. Before joining any organization, ask yourself whether you are really fit for this job or not? It is always better to do your home work carefully rather than repenting later.

You need to slightly change your attitude as well. Do not have unrealistic expectations. Do not expect your Boss to treat you the way your mother does. It cannot be possible. Why do you expect your superiors to call you and enquire about your health if you have applied for sick leaves? Do not expect your organization to give you five days leaves just because you have planned a trip with your girlfriend. Please do not try to be too personal with your reporting Boss. Understand the difference between your office and home. At work, you can't have the comforts of home. If your boss wants you to go for an urgent meeting on a holiday, please do not get upset or demotivated. Moreover, would cribbing solve your problem? I don't think it would. Then what is the point reacting? Accept challenges with a smile. You can't say a NO always in your job. As long as you are associated with an organization, you are bound to listen to your reporting bosses and adhere to the rules and regulations. It is always better to accept challenges with a smile rather than getting demotivated and look for a new job every time. After all, how many jobs would you change? Believe me, there would be a problem everywhere. Remember, if you can't change others, it is always better to change yourself. Not everyone would behave the way you like. Would you change your job just because your team member is irritating and you do not like him? Do not interfere much in other's lives. Concentrate more on your work rather than your colleague's.

Leave your ego behind the moment you enter the workplace. Do you have to create an issue if once you receive your incentives a little late? Do not be too rigid. Learn to cooperate with the management as well as people around. Flash your smile quite often. Remember, fighting and indulging in conflicts yield no solution, rather create more problems for you. The mantra for a peaceful life is to be neither too possessive for your job nor take it too lightly. Do not attend official calls after 7pm unless and until it is too urgent. If you do not enjoy your personal life, believe me, you will never be satisfied with your job. Learn to take things lightly.

www.ingramcontent.com/pod-product-compliance
Lightning Source LLC
Chambersburg PA
CBHW080826180526
45168CB00006B/2588